Chaotic and Critically Damaged

Nymeria Publishing LLC

First published in the United States of America by Nymeria Publishing
LLC, 2021

Nymeria Publishing
PO Box 85981
Lexington, SC 29073
Visit our website at www.nymeriapublishing.com

ISBN 978-7363027-0-5

Printed in U.S.A
Illustrations by Neph

For the Warriors, the Survivors,
and those still trying to find their voice

Table of Contents

Chapter One
This Body is No Longer a Home

I always said I loved the silence
But the truth is my mind is always screaming so loudly trying to persuade my lips to move
But my lips can never seem to coordinate so I end up babbling like a baboon
I always said I'd be a writer
But when a pen and paper wouldn't do, I took to my wrists
With a razor as the pen and my blood as the ink
I wrote down the bad days
But I could never show anyone my work because of creative differences
You see society doesn't take kindly to the damaged
So on the good days I'd cover my wrists with my sleeves praying to the God I don't believe in that no one would ask me to pull them up
I always said I was happy
But that wasn't exactly the truth
You see what I actually meant to say was that I got out of bed today and that was the only reason I could think to fake this smile
I always said this would be the last time I tried
But I think we both knew that soon the pills sitting on my desk would start whispering their sweet nothings to draw me back again
Maybe if I stay in bed, I won't be able to reach the bottle
I always said I knew you cared
But when I tried to show you my stories you gawked at me like I was an animal on display
You tried to put me in a hospital so you wouldn't have to see my pain
Soon the whole family knew I was show stopping sight
The girl who tried to kill herself
Step up one step up all get your tickets to the show while she's still alive
Every family get-together turned into my funeral
People talking about me like I was already dead
I always said I was trying to get better
And the truth is that was the one time I wasn't lying

K. L. Champitto

It isn't really a specific point on my map
More like a route
I haven't successfully taken yet

K. L. Champitto

This body is no longer a home
But a resting place
For a lost soul

K. L. Champitto

That moment when you can feel your heart shattering
But not all at once
No
It's slow and painful
You can feel each individual piece breaking off
Falling into the pit of your stomach
Filling you up so much that when they ask you why you
aren't eating, and you tell them you're full
You aren't lying
You want to scream but you can't
The demons inside you have scratched your throat raw carving the
words "I'm okay" into your voice box repeatedly until those are the
only words you know how to say
Instead of makeup every morning you paint on a brave face
A face that shines with the confidence you pretend to have
But the paint isn't waterproof
The first mean word thrown at you splashes against your face
like raindrops washing away your war paint
Sooner or later, you waste away into the floor that every single person
that has hurt you walks upon
Their actions push into your skin like footprints until you are so
unrecognizable that you don't even see yourself anymore when you
look in the mirror
You let out screams and you are left to wonder if they didn't hear you
or if they are just standing there
Praying they aren't next

K. L. Champitto

I told you I was fine
When I was already buried
6ft underground

K. L. Champitto

Not yet broken
But no longer working
No longer dreaming
But not yet done breathing

K. L. Champitto

Now it just hollows me out a little more
Each time I drink I lose a little piece of me I didn't know I had
But drinking makes the girl in the mirror my friend instead of my
enemy
It makes her smile
She doesn't do that very often

K. L. Champitto

I'm just an Alice who fell down the wrong rabbit hole
I'm the only mad one here

K. L. Champitto

With nowhere else to go
I shook death's hand
But it wasn't my time yet
He tipped his hood
"Until we meet again"

K. L. Champitto

I've always been known to overindulge
I never really know when to stop
I'm the kind of person who will eat an entire box of cookies in one
sitting all while watching every episode of my favorite show
Even though I've already seen all 400 episodes
Twice
And I don't even like the kind of cookies I'm eating
You see I can't really trust myself
I'm not so good at not doing things I shouldn't
Like staying up all night even though I know I work the morning shift
the next day
Or eating an entire tub of ice cream even though I know I'll probably
throw it up in the next 5 minutes
Or taking an entire bottle of pills knowing I won't die
But also knowing I'll wake up the next morning really wishing I was
dead
When was little I would eat the chocolate from the candy dish in my
grandmothers living room
I was always told to take one
But instead, I would eat as many as I wanted hiding the wrappers in
the couch cushions
For some reason my 4-year-old self didn't think they would notice the
empty bowl
After a while they stopped filling it
In the same way my psychiatrist told me next time I want to overdose
to give my pills to a friend
Basically, reassuring me that I'm not to be trusted with my own life
But then again if you handed me a gun, I would probably shoot myself
Even though I've never shot a gun and never plan to
They terrify me
So I guess I see her point
Like I said I can't trust myself
So next time I think about killing myself
I think I'll give you my bottle of pills
And I'll just take a box of cookies

K. L. Champitto

I was told to be happy
To see nothing but blue skies
But blue is also the color of rain
And there is much more beauty in the storm

K. L. Champitto

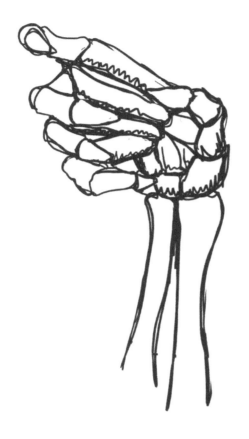

Someone once asked me if I was afraid to die
If I was afraid, I would end up in Hell
I only smiled
For I have been in Hell my whole life

K. L. Champitto

My favorite color used to be yellow
But now it's black
And I can't help but see the irony in that
Like I'm some sort of sunflower
Someone forgot to water along the way
But still cared enough to leave me out in the sun
So I could grow
You see I'm missing all of my petals
So no one ever really picks me
And I don't know if that's a blessing or a curse
Because flowers that are picked will eventually die
But maybe I want to die
Because how do they expect me to live
When I've lost all of my leaves
How do they expect me to live
If I can't even perform photosynthesis
And by photosynthesis I actually mean taking care of myself
Because sometimes I don't eat for days
And it's not because I don't want to
But because I can't get myself out of bed
My roots only extend as far as the bathroom
And sometimes even that's too far
My life isn't pretty
It isn't a meadow
The wildfire already came through here
Maybe it's still coming through here
Maybe it never really stops coming through here
Maybe I wished it did
My favorite color used to be yellow
Because it was painted on the walls of my bedroom
Because it peaked through the cracks in my window
Because I saw it in my reflection when I smiled
I don't see it anymore
And I can't help
But see the irony in that

K. L. Champitto

I don't like the word today
Or the word tomorrow
Or yesterday
Maybe I just don't like words
But how can that be when I'm a writer
Maybe I just don't like words that make me feel guilty
Like the words for the days of the week
Because each day is just another reminder
Of how I don't feel worth it

K. L. Champitto

I inherited my brown eyes
From my mother
My quiet from my father
And my laughter from my sister
I inherited my tears from the sky
Because maybe it wasn't blue enough
Or maybe I just couldn't see it
My parents may have given me bad eyes
But it was the world that made me blind

K. L. Champitto

Chapter Two
Leave the Light on if You Go

He didn't say, "I don't love you anymore"
He said, "I think we need a break"
He said, "We are growing apart"
"These things take time"
"We're just not right"
"I can't do this anymore"
He didn't say, "I don't love you anymore"
But he didn't have to

K. L. Champitto

I was once known as the lionhearted girl
Fierce and vibrant
He took that with him the day he left

K. L. Champitto

He smelled like coffee and bad decisions
But maybe that's what I needed

K. L. Champitto

I've never really believed in love
But my heart beat a little faster every time you looked at me
When you spoke, I followed each word into the darkness
Your voice was the only flashlight I needed
I clung to your every word, never knowing when it would be the last
that I would hear
Your breath was the Oxygen keeping me alive
You were my everything
What I didn't realize was that you were a thief
Slowly stealing pieces of me so that I wouldn't notice
You took my smile first
Removing one tooth at a time until my mouth was bare and I had
nothing left to show
You stole the light in my eyes
Blowing out the candles of my passions
The world doesn't look the same anymore
You stole my reflection
Now every time I look in the mirror all I see is the skeleton of a girl that
once existed
So unrecognizable that it seems as though I am looking at another
person
When I met you I was stranded in the void of my mind
I was folded so far within myself
I had almost given up
I had almost turned my back on the world
You appeared as an angel equipped with strong arms and easy eyes
Held me so tight
Told me I mattered
I hadn't heard that before
But then left me as if I never even meant anything to you at all
When you met me I was trying to find myself and I found it within
you
You took it with you the day you left
I may never get it back
You left me chaotic and critically damaged
I'm stuck on life support
And I'm ready for you to pull the plug

K. L. Champitto

It's okay if you don't love me
But please leave the light on if you go
Leave the door cracked
Leave the space that once existed between us
So I know something about this was real

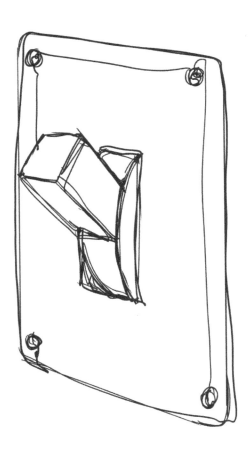

K. L. Champitto

I always thought you spoke so little
But now I know
Your silence spoke too many words
Your closed eyes took too many glances
Your absence took too many pieces
Leaving my soul no longer whole

K. L. Champitto

I wish to be seen
With more than your eyes
For my life is worth more
Than the shade you see me in

K. L. Champitto

I've always tried to not depend on another person because I knew deep
down that they would eventually leave
But when you waltzed into my life I began to wonder if maybe you
would stick around
When I met you I was an injured deer who had fallen into your trap
Your words slipped into my empty spaces making me feel whole again
I should have known better
Because words can disguise themselves
They can turn a raindrop into a thunderstorm
I was a hurricane and you were the eye of my storm
The calm before the madness
You were the tease of a better life
I thought if I meant something to you then it would feel like my choice
this time
But you threw me away so quickly as if I had never really meant
anything at all
I felt like an empty casing, a shell
For the bright-eyed outspoken girl that fled the scene was no longer a
part of me
Now I am left as damaged goods
Labeled fragile so everyone is left scared to touch me
Nobody loves a broken girl
You took away the part of me I had left to give
You smashed it into a million pieces
You can't fix a broken heart with duct tape
But lord knows I have tried
I want to not be afraid to let this fairy tale become reality
I'm afraid because my dreams always seem to evolve into nightmares
and I never seem to survive those
I'm in this constant state of limbo
Never knowing what is real and what is imaginary
Never knowing whether my eyes are closed or opened

K. L. Champitto

Chapter Three
Destined to Drown

I never wanted to write about you

K. L. Champitto

I have never felt more empty
Than with a dead life
Inside of me

K. L. Champitto

I will never get to say hello
Or see your face
I will never get to hold you
Or tell you that everything will be okay

K. L. Champitto

Am I destined to drown
If I sink my ship
Before it even begins to float

K. L. Champitto

A single voice
Can bring back memories
Memories of a dark room
A scream
And a few bruises

K. L. Champitto

I wonder if you stay up at night thinking about all the things you've
done
If your words, that are still seared into my skin, are traced on the backs
of your eyelids
If when you close your eyes, they hurt you now, as much as they hurt
me then
If my skin is still underneath your fingernails
If your ears are still burning from my no's
I wonder what the hell happened to you
If your life was so awful, you had to throw mine into the fire
If your reflection was so far gone, you had to make mine disappear too
If hate was the only thing wired into your brain from day one
I wonder if I would hate you a little less if that were true
Because it's easy to hate a monster
It's easy to cast them aside as the bad guy
Because that's all you ever were to me
I wonder if you take pills every day
If you keep your closet doors closed at night to keep the demons from
escaping
If it takes every ounce of your strength to get out of bed in the morning
If you paint on your self-confidence, hoping to cast a better reflection
Because I do
Sometimes I wonder if we could have been friends
If you had used your words as a life preserver
Instead of putting them into a revolver, like bullets
Shooting me down every chance you got
If you had faced your monsters
Instead of becoming one yourself
Sometimes I wonder if I ever pop into your mind
If my impact in your life was as big as the one you had on me
If I left a hole in your memories too
Or if you're still digging your grave
Burying all the things you've done with you

K. L. Champitto

Your words leave ghosts
            To haunt me

K. L. Champitto

My nightmares roll through
Like thunderstorms
Flooding my brain

K. L. Champitto

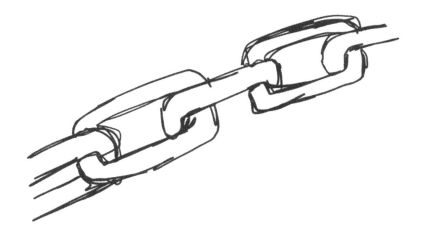

I carry you with me
Through each day
Even as you shackle me to the ground

K. L. Champitto

When the memories start to flood back
I find myself drowning
But it's not like I just fell into the water
I've been standing in it for years

K. L. Champitto

My body is still a crime scene
Except I put up the caution tape

K. L. Champitto

Chapter Four
No One is Beyond Repair

Be still
Let darkness be darkness
Sometimes a heartbeat
Is just that

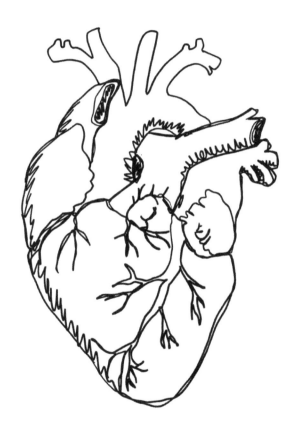

K. L. Champitto

Would you still find me beautiful, if you knew about all
the pain I've caused
If you saw all the scars I hide
If you heard all of the tears, I've cried
Would you still find my words poetic, if you knew they were written in
my blood
If you saw me carving them into my skin
If you heard me scream as I tried
Would you still be able to look at me the same, if you knew

K. L. Champitto

I don't want a cure
I don't want a sunrise mind
I want to live in my twilight
But know that it isn't my only home
I want to get better
But I don't want to lose myself by doing it
I don't want to silence my demons
I want to become their friend
To become their equal
They don't own these vocal cords
But then again neither do I
We are both living in this body
We might as well learn how to share
I don't want to make sense to the world
I just want to make sense to myself
To not lose the mind that was gifted to me
We are only given one life
I don't want to give mine up anymore
Maybe I never did in the first place
Maybe I just wanted to be free
Maybe
Just maybe, I could be

K. L. Champitto

I gave you life
And I think
Even if only for second
You gave me life too

K. L. Champitto

Our love is quietly beautiful
The kind that sneaks up on you
The kind that doesn't come with an explanation
The kind that doesn't need one

K. L. Champitto

I am sorry that I don't talk much
But you are dealing with a girl who has spent most of her life getting
told to stay quiet that I'm so scared I'll drive you away with my words
I was broken
I am broken
I may always be broken because not everything that falls apart can be
put back together
I'm sorry that I'm broken
I never meant for you to have to pick up the pieces, but please don't
take any if you leave me
So many already have
I'm the puzzle you buy at the garage sale
I'm missing a few pieces, but I swear if you take the time to put me
together you will see that I can still be beautiful despite my flaws
I'm sorry that I will get jealous
Although I will never admit it, my eyes will tell it all
And it's not because I don't trust you, but because so many people have
taught me that I am replaceable and that's a lesson I will never forget
I'm sorry that I will have my bad days
Days where I can't get out of bed
Days where I have to continuously count the reasons to stay alive
Days where I don't have any reasons to count
These are the days I will need you to hold me close
You don't have to say a word, your presence will be my armor
Protecting me from the dangers inside of my head
I'm sorry that I will have my good days
Days where all I want to do is dance around a room singing at the top
of my lungs
Days where I want to go for walks that never end
Days where I will laugh at the smallest things
These are days I will need you to laugh along with me
These are days I will need you to remember me, because this is who I
really am
But don't be fooled into thinking I am better
I'm sorry for the days I seem distant
Sometimes I get lost in my head
On these days I don't need you to be my knight in shining armor
On these days I need you to let me fix myself
I am sorry I will need you in ways other people will not
But I promise if you stick around this could be something beautiful

K. L. Champitto

"What becomes of the broken hearted?"
She whispers
I sigh
"They become stronger"

K. L. Champitto

Why must I grow small
For the world around me
To grow bigger

K. L. Champitto

He could never tell her
She was the first thing he thought of when he woke up
Or that she was his life jacket
When the rest of the world was trying to drown him
He could never tell her he needed her
But she already knew
And she needed him too

K. L. Champitto

I sometimes wish I was normal
But then I remember
How lonely I am
When the voices in my head
Aren't speaking to me

K. L. Champitto

It's okay to be proud of the little things
Some days those are the only things you can manage

K. L. Champitto

When I have a child their first word will be love
Because love is the most powerful thing in the world but we sometimes forget how to use it
Their first toy will be a flashlight so that they will grow up knowing that there will always be a light in the darkness
Their first book will be empty for I want them to fill it with their own stories
Be their own hero, their own happy ending
When I have a child I will teach them to color outside of the lines
To not let society tell them which crayon is the blue or the pink one
I want them to decide that for themselves
When I have a child they will be encouraged to explore their imaginations
That they hold the world in their hands
That they are capable of anything
I will not let the world crush their dreams before they've even begun forming
When I have a child I will show them that razors are not meant to draw blood
I will instead teach them to punch a pillow because some destruction is good just not the destruction of themselves or of others
And when they are stranded in their own minds I will send out compassion disguised as search teams to bring them back for the mind can be a lonely place I do not want them to find solace in
When I have a child and they go through their first break up I will hug them
I will hand them a tub of ice cream and two spoons
I will not let them be alone
I will not tell them to put on a brave face or a false smile
When I have a child I will teach them to embrace their emotions
That holding everything in will start to strip you down until you are nothing but a faded image of the person you once were
I will teach them to let things go
To never hold a grudge
When I have a child I will tell them that their mother was once broken too
But everyone can be fixed
No one is beyond repair

K. L. Champitto

I wish I could go back in time
Tell myself that it's going to be okay
That someday a man will find me beautiful
And teach me what it truly means to be in love

K. L. Champitto

CPSIA information can be obtained
at www.ICGtesting.com
Printed in the USA
BVHW042148270821
615503BV00013B/385